S0-DFH-548

CREATIVE

DRIED & SILK
FLOWER ARRANGING

Text and Floral Designs: Ming Veevers-Carter, Jane Newdick
Photography: Neil Sutherland, Steve Tanner
Design: Lindsey Philpott and Natasha Waters, Art of Design
Editor: Laura Potts

CHARTWELL BOOKS
A division of Book Sales, Inc.
POST OFFICE BOX 7100
114 Northfield Avenue
Edison, N.J. 08818-7100

CLB 3362

Author's Acknowledgements
Topher Faulkner, Hannah Catling, Cherry Clark, Caroline Little,
Angela Chamberlain, Vanessa Lee, Sarah Eastwood, Donna Henderson,
Francis Bearman and Jo Finnis.
Dried flowers: *Robson Whatley*, *R& R Flowers*, *Machin & Henry*, *Tudor Rose*.
Silk Flowers: *Best Blooms*, *H Andreas*, *Austin & Co*, *Forever Flowers*.
Sundries: *Cocquerels* and *Peter Harvey*.

All products used in this book are available from Veevers Carter Flowers,
125 Sydney Street, London SW3, tel: 071 370 0549

CREATIVE

DRIED & SILK
FLOWER ARRANGING

CHARTWELL
BOOKS, INC.

Introduction

*F*or many years thought of as second-best to fresh flowers, dried and silk flowers are at last beginning to be recognised in their own right. With dried flowers, methods of preserving have greatly improved and commercial drieds are now strong in colour and form. Availability as well as quality has improved and a range of outlets, from specialist shops to garden centres, now supply a wide variety of drieds. These blooms can be used to make stunning designs and can be used in a number of ways. Silk flowers have also improved in quality and are now so realistic they can be substituted into an arrangement of fresh flowers, with few people able to tell the difference.

Yet, even with such an abundance, many people shy away from working with dried and artificial flowers. This reluctance may in part stem from a lack of knowledge of how to prepare and work with them. This book is intended to act as a practical guide, enabling the reader to create professional displays every time. It gives step-by-step instructions on how to create the arrangements, explaining each stage of preparation and giving a whole host of useful tips on how to get the best from the flowers.

Arrangements do not have to be elaborate to give maximum effect, and often simple, well-planned displays can have the most impact. The arrangements in this book show the versatility of dried and silk flowers, showing how they can be used to create gifts, ornaments and table decorations. The book will act as an inspiration for the experienced flower arranger and will give encouragement to the beginner.

Drying Flowers

Commercially dried flowers are usually bought in bunches of one type, though from certain outlets it is possible to buy mixed bunches. When buying, check the bunch to make sure that the flowers are in good condition. Start by checking their colour to make sure that it is still strong, comparing blooms to ensure that they have not faded. Once satisfied with the colour of the flowers, take the bunch, turn it upside down very carefully and shake it gently to make sure that the flowers are not brittle or damaged. The dried cones, seedheads and pods, which often form an important part of an arrangement, can be bought singly, as can artificial flowers and paper flowers

Flowers can also be dried effectively at home. The most common method of drying flowers, and the one that is used commercially, is air-drying. The flowers are grouped together in small bunches and are bound together tightly near the end of the stem with an elastic band. An elastic band, rather than string, is used as it shrinks with the stems as they dry. The flowers are then hung up to dry in a dark, warm, well-ventilated room for a few days. The plants should be completely dry before they are used – a length of time that varies from plant to plant. For the best results the flowers to be dried should be harvested on a dry day, when all the dew has evaporated.

Air-drying, though cheap and easy, is not suitable for all flowers and other drying methods have to be employed for some plants. Roses, peonies, lilies, freesia, fuschia and anemones, for example, should be dried with a desiccant like sand, borax or silica gel. Silica gel, usually available from chemists or hardware shops as white crystals, is the most effective method, though it is also the most expensive. The flowers that are to be dried are placed on a layer of the crystals in a container and are very carefully covered with more crystals. The sealed container is then left for approximately 48 hours in a warm place. Often the dried flowers are quite brittle so great care has to be taken when removing them from the container. Borax works on the same principal and is far cheaper, though the drying process is longer, taking approximately 10 days.

Deciduous and evergreen foliage is preserved in glycerine. The stems to be dried are stood in a shallow depth, approximately 8-10 cm (3-4 in), of glycerine solution for at least a week. This solution, made up of one part glycerine to two parts water, will gradually replace the water in the leaves.

Tools

To be successful in arranging dried flowers a few basic tools are needed. A good pair of scissors are essential and, if you are going to use flowers with thick stems, a pair of secateurs are also valuable. You should be equipped with a sharp knife with which to cut florist's foam, a large reel of sticky tape and some thin wire mesh. A glue gun, which can be used to glue all kinds of items onto wreaths, baskets, wood and fabric, is also a very useful tool. It should, however, be used with care, as the glue is very hot and can easily burn your fingers.

The mechanics, or the methods by which an arrangement is supported, in dried flower arranging are similar to those used in fresh flower arranging. In smaller arrangements dry florist's foam is used as the basis, while in larger displays that require more support heavier wire mesh is used. In arranging dried flowers, however, a great deal more preparation is needed for the individual blooms. Often when a flower has been dried its stem may be too thick or too brittle to be arranged successfully and it will need to be wired. There are many types of wire that are available. For most work, four kinds of wire – narrow and thick silver wire, 22 gauge stem wire and 18 gauge stem wire – will be sufficient.

Silver florist's wire, also known as rose wire, should be used to wire single blooms for use in delicate work such as small posies and garlands. Although fine, this wire is firm enough to take the weight of small flowers. Begin by cutting the flowers from stems. Hold the flower head firmly between thumb and forefinger. Make a loop in a length of wire and hold under the short stem. Then wind one end around the length of stem about 6 times keeping the wire taut.

The 18 or 22 gauge stem wires are used to wire flowers singly or in bunches, for use in large arrangements. The 18 gauge stem wire is the stronger of the two and should be used only if the wire is to be the only support for the bunch. The 22 gauge stem wire is suitable for mounting bunches onto canes. To wire a bunch of dried flowers, take a few stems and cut them to the required length - usually 12.5-17.5 cm (5-7 in). Hold the stems together tightly at the bottom between thumb and forefinger. Bend the stem wire two-thirds of the way along its length to form a loop, then place the loop against the stems of the bunch, holding it in place with the third finger. Twist the longer portion of the wire around the bunch. The wire should be tight enough to hold the stems securely but not so tight that it damages them.

Florist's tape is used to cover the wires supporting the flowers, making them less visible in a finished arrangement. To cover the wire with tape, start from the top, near the flower head and work diagonally downwards. Begin by holding the wire between the thumb and forefinger. Then, holding the tape at right angles to the wire and pulling it slightly to keep it taught, begin to cover the wire. As you proceed, twist the wire rather than the tape, making sure that the tape overlaps slightly.

Simple Arrangements & Gift Ideas

*G*ifts can be given a personal touch by gluing dried flowers – either single heads or bunches – onto giftwrap or decorative ribbon.

Gift Basket with Roses

This romantic heart-shaped basket filled with fragrant pot-pourri makes a memorable gift.

You will need:

30-35 roses
2 heads hydrangea
2 m (2¼ yd) wire-edged ribbon

Instructions

Line a heart-shaped wicker basket with plastic to prevent any essential oils in the pot-pourri from seeping through the basket onto the table and then cover this with material, gluing it into place. Take the wire-edged ribbon and glue it onto the basket, creating a scrunched effect as you go. If you are using a glue gun, squeeze a small amount of glue onto the basket, wait a few seconds, then press the ribbon onto glue, so avoiding any risk of burning your fingers. Remove the stems from the roses entirely. Squeeze a little glue onto the underside of each rose and hold in place on the basket until the glue dries. When finished, remove any strands of glue. Fill basket with hydrangea florets and add a few drops of essential oil if desired.

Pomanders

These delightful rose-covered balls are quite simple to make and when they are grouped together they make a very effective display.

You will need:

2 bunches roses

Instructions

Trim the rose stems, leaving 2.5 cm (1 in) in length. Choose a foam ball of the required size and hold it in the palm of the hand. Push the roses into the foam, keeping them close together. Once one side of the ball is completed, turn it over and very gently continue inserting the roses into the other side until it is covered.

Napkin Decoration

These beautifully-presented napkins make an unusual decoration for a celebration table.

You will need:

A selection of flowerheads and cones
Wire-edged ribbon

Instructions

Use wire edged ribbon to create a lavish bow. Then attach a single dried flower or a selection of pretty cones to this with a little wire. The colour and textures of the flowers should coordinate with the overall colour scheme of the table.

Bottle with Garland

Bring an extra touch of magic to a special occasion with an attractive garland of small, brightly-coloured flowers.

You will need:

8 red roses
2 stems larkspur
1 bunch globe amaranth
1 bunch small-flowered achillea

Instructions

Choose a selection of flowers, ensuring that they work well together before beginning to wire them. Wire the flowers with silver wires (page 11) and cover the wires with stem binding tape (page 11). Bend an 18 gauge wire into a hoop, overlap the ends and twist them together. Cover with stem binding tape. Bind the flowers onto the hoop one at a time, making 3 or 4 twists, then trimming the excess wire. Continue until the hoop is full. Attaching the final flower to the circlet may be tricky. Begin by pulling the other flowers out of the way slightly, then wire on the last flower, rearranging the others when this has been done.

Hat with Garland

Bright helichrysum *and* helipterum *are used to decorate the crown of a straw hat, making a pretty dried flower decoration. A big red bow provides definition to the finished arrangement.*

You will need:

1 bunch *helichrysum*
1 bunch *helipterum*
1 head hydrangea
1 m (1⅛ yd) satin ribbon

Instructions

Use reel wire to bind together small, tight bunches, mixing the flowers. It is advisable to make more than you think that you are going to need, as when the garland is wound around the hat a few empty areas may appear. Cut a piece of string long enough to wind around the crown of the hat, making sure that there is sufficient to tie the ends. Lay the bunches out along the piece of string before beginning to ensure that the colours are spread evenly. Then attach some reel wire to the string, about 10 cm (4 in) from the end. Position one of the small bunches over the join and wind the wire around the stems to attach it firmly to the string. Wire overlapping bunches along the string, until the desired length is reached. Cut and secure the wire. Tie the garland around the hat and use the spare bunches of flowers to fill any gaps, securing them with wire. Once happy with the overall look of the display, cut off the ends of string. Tie a large red bow and glue it to the hat, covering the join.

Victorian Posy

Quite a high degree of skill is needed to create this formal,
Victorian-style posy, but the finished result, a colourful, fragrant arrangement, is well
worth the effort.

You will need:
2 bunches marjoram
2 bunches lavender
27 orange roses, one large
20 red roses

Instructions

Prepare the flowers before beginning, wiring the roses singly and the marjoram and lavender in small bunches (page 11). Cover the wires with stem binding tape. Start with the large rose in the centre and surround it with marjoram. The bunches should be clustered together quite tightly and should be positioned slightly lower than the central bud. Bind the stems together with silver reel wire where your hand is holding the bouquet. Then add the next set of flowers, again making sure that they are positioned slightly lower than the preceding circle. Wire the stems as you go along, making a central handle for the posy. Continue to add the flowers in this way, turning the posy as you work. Look at the side of the posy occasionally to make sure that it is taking on a domed shape. When complete, trim wire stems and bind with tape (page 11). To finish cover handle with ribbon .To do this take a length of ribbon, hold it to the top of the handle and run it downwards over the bottom of the handle, then upwards to the top of the handle. With the other hand, wrap the uncut ribbon down the handle. Then work upwards to the handle top and tie the ribbon onto the free length. Make a simple bow and tie to the top of the handle with a double knot. Insert a long pin into the centre of the bow to secure it.

Baskets

*W*hat better way to bring year-round cheer to a room than to decorate it with a small basket of dried flowers. These arrangements, though they take time to prepare, are relatively simple to put together.

Round Basket

This delightful basket combines many different colours and textures.

You will need:

2 bunches lavender
1 bunch red roses
1 bunch marjoram
1 bunch *Eucalyptus*
1 bunch orange *Helichrysum*
7 open roses

Instructions

Wire the roses, *Helichrysum* and *Eucalyptus* in groups of three stems and the marjoram and lavender in small bunches (page 11), using 22 gauge wire. Bind the wires with tape (page 11). Then cut a block of foam slightly bigger than the basket, trim the corners and fit it into place. Cover the foam lightly with moss. Cut a piece of wire netting slightly smaller than the basket and use it to cover the moss, attaching it at intervals to the rim of the basket with black reel wire. Position bunches of either lavender and marjoram all over the foam, using them to create the basic shape of the arrangement. Then add the remaining flowers, creating a mixed yet even effect. Once the arrangement is complete, bend the bunches downwards so that they cover the edge.

Wedding Basket

Roses, peonies, hydrangea and cow parsley have been combined to make a romantic basket that is ideal for a wedding.

You will need:
1 bunch cow parsley
30 stems dark red roses ('Jaguar')
6 stems miniature pink species roses ('Pink Delight')
6 peonies
2 heads hydrangea

Instructions

Cut a block of foam slightly bigger than the basket, trim the corners and fit it into place. Cover the foam lightly with moss. Cut a piece of wire netting slightly smaller than the basket and use it to cover the moss, attaching it at intervals to the rim of the basket with black reel wire. Wire the roses into small bunches. Push the bunches into the foam, using them to create the basic shape of the arrangement. Then wire the remaining flowers and add them to the display, creating a mixed yet even effect. Once the arrangement is complete, bend the bunches downwards so that they cover the edge of the basket.

Bouquets

$\mathcal{W}$hen they are packed with a variety of colourful blooms and secured with a lavish, ornamental bow, simple bouquets can be spectacular.

This extravagant bouquet of dried summer blooms can be hung on a wall or door for all to admire.

Summer Bouquet with Bow

You will need:

2 bunches marjoram
2 bunches *Ageratum*
1 bunch green golden rod
1 bunch *Achillea*
20 roses
7 peonies
3 heads hydrangea
1 m (1⅛) x 30 cm (12 in) wide silk

Instructions

Begin by making the bow. Cut a strip of silk about 10 cm (4 in) in depth from the shorter side of the piece and set it aside. This will be used later to make the 'knot' in the middle of the bow. Fold in about 2.5 cm (1 in) lengthways down each side of the fabric, then fold in half, bringing the two hemmed edges together, and glue. Cut the short ends diagonally, turn under the raw edges and glue. Make the bow and secure with 22 gauge stem wire around the middle. To make the 'knot', take the remaining strip of silk, fold in a hem of approximately 2.5 cm (1 in) lengthways down each side. Then fold, overlapping the hemmed edges slightly in the middle, and glue. Try to use the glue sparingly so

that it does not seep through the fabric. Tie this strip around the wire fixing the bow and glue into place. Cut away any excess material.

Wire two peonies singly and the remaining five into small bunches with a selection of other flowers, and set these aside. Then in one hand gather up a few stems at a time and wire together just below the hand. Continue adding stems, reducing the length of extending stems. Secure them with wire. Then fix the pre-prepared bow to the front of the bouquet with wire. Slide in the wired stems and the small bunches just above the bow, bending them forward slightly. These should give the bouquet extra fullness.

Wreaths & Garlands

$\mathcal{W}$reaths can be constructed in several ways. The easiest way is to use one of the pre-prepared dry foam rings that are widely available. When using one of these rings it is important to cover it amply, as any uncovered areas of foam that are visible in the final arrangement will spoil the overall effect. Alternatively, intertwined branches can be used to form the basis of the wreath.

Autumn Wreath

Dried woodland items and Eucalyptus *have been combined with purple ribbon to make a spectacular autumnal wreath.*

You will need:

1 straw ring 35 cm (14 in) in diameter
5 bunches assorted dried woodland items,
eg cones, tree mushrooms etc
2 bunches dried *Eucalyptus*
12 proteas
4-5 m (4½-5½ yd) wire-edged ribbon

Instructions

Bind an 18 gauge wire with stem binding tape and attach to the straw ring. Wind the wire around the wreath once only, then twist the ends together tightly, so that it cannot move around the ring. Cut the ends, leaving enough wire to be able to attach it to a curtain rail. Wire the selection of dried woodland items into bunches of 3 and bind with tape (page 11). Cut *Eucalyptus* into 10-12 cm (4-5 in) long pieces. Cut proteas, leaving a stub of stem, approximately 7.5 cm (3 in) in

length. Attach a strong piece of twine to the ring to bind the flowers onto it. Place a few stems of *Eucalyptus* onto ring and bind tightly with twine keeping it taught at all times. Add a couple of proteas, bind tightly then add a woodland bunch. Bind tightly once more. Continue until ring is covered. Make 9 small double-looped bows and 1 large bow for the top. Attach 22 gauge stem wires to the bows and then insert them into wreath at intervals.

Woodland Wreath

You will need:

1 foam ring 30 cm (12 in) in diameter
3 bunches of grasses
1 bunch blue larkspur
1 bunch *Alchemilla*
20 stems roses
20 tree mushrooms
6 artificial mushrooms
3 heads hydrangea

Both dried tree mushrooms and artificial mushrooms have been used to create this lovely woodland wreath.

Instructions

Cut a piece of fabric to cover the base of the foam ring, ensuring that it is slightly larger than the ring itself. Apply the glue to the reverse of the fabric and press it firmly into place. It should cover the sides of the ring to a level of 1 cm (½ in). If you are using a glue gun be very careful not to burn your fingers. Wire the roses, larkspur, grasses and *Alchemilla* into small bunches. Break the hydrangea heads into segments and wire each individually, making a hook with stub wire, threading it carefully through the piece and binding the ends with reel wire. Wire the tree mushrooms, very carefully threading a piece of wire

horizontally through the stem just beneath the cap, leaving an equal amount of wire on both sides. Gently bend the two pieces of wire to make an inverted v-shape. Cover the wires of the prepared material with stem binding tape (page 11). Trim the wires slightly so that they do not pierce the underside of wreath when mounted. Remember that wires of marginally different lengths will make a more interesting arrangement, giving texture and depth. Starting at the top of the foam ring, begin to construct the wreath, pushing the wires firmly into the foam, creating a pattern of colour as you work.

Herb Wreath

This fragrant, colourful wreath is made from culinary herbs and would make an ideal present for any enthusiastic cook.

You will need:

1 twig ring
1 bunch fresh rosemary
1 bunch marjoram
5 bushy stems fresh bay
70 dried chillies

Instructions

Begin by trimming the stems of the marjoram and rosemary to 17.5 cm (7 in) in length. The stems of the bay leaves can be cut shorter. Using silver reel wire, wire together bunches of chillies. Wire these bunches with 22 gauge stem wires and bind with stem binding tape (page 11). If the wreath is to be hung, attach the wire at this stage, before beginning the arrangement. To do this, cover a piece of wire with stem binding tape and then wrap it around the wreath. Then, to ensure that this does not slip, twist the wire together tightly. Leave the ends of the wire long enough to be twisted into a hook. If the wreath is particularly heavy, use two pieces of wire bound together, to give it more support. Begin the arrangement by positioning one of the bunches of marjoram on the ring and securing it with wire. Add the chillies, bay and then rosemary, making sure that they are positioned quite close together. Repeat the pattern until the wreath is complete.

Table Arrangements

*T*hese clever combinations of dried flowers and candles make sophisticated decorations that will bring warmth to your table.

Candle Group

Bring a warm glow to your winter table with this small arrangement.

You will need:
2 bunches woodland cones
1 bunch green marjoram
1 bunch marjoram
20 stems red species roses ('Nikita')
20 stems yellow roses ('Golden Times')
6 narrow beeswax candles

Instructions
Fill the container with foam, cover with moss and tape in place. Insert two pieces of green cane into the bottom of each candle, ensuring that they are not pushed in further than 2.5 cm (1 in). Group the candles in the centre of the foam. Wire dried items in bunches, grouping four or five together at a time. Cover the wires with stem binding tape. Push the bunches firmly into the foam, making a 'collar' around the candles, mixing the colours and textures well. Bend the lower bunches well down over the container's edge to soften the effect.

Beeswax Candle

*The warm, muted colours of
this arrangement make it immediately
attractive. It is ideal as a table decoration
or as an ornament for a bedroom.*

You will need:

2 bunches marjoram
1 bunch globe amaranth
1 bunch green golden rod
20 red roses
15 open peach roses
1 chunky beeswax candle

Instructions

Pack a low container with a piece of foam, making sure that it sits about 2.5 cm (1 in) higher than the rim. Cover the foam with moss and use florist's tape to secure it. Begin by positioning the beeswax candle in the centre of the foam. With a thick candle, it is a good idea to make cane 'legs' rather than inserting the cane directly into the base of the candle. To do this cut three 10 cm (4 in) pieces of cane. Hold one piece against the side of the candle and secure it with green adhesive tape. Do the same with the two remaining pieces of cane, creating a three-legged support. Once all three pieces are in position, wind adhesive tape round a few more times to hold it firmly. Wire the marjoram, globe amaranth and green golden rod into small bunches and the roses singly (page 11). Bind all the stems with stem binding tape. Insert bunches of marjoram all over the foam, using them to create the basic shape of the arrangement. Fill in with the remainder of the flowers, pushing them deeper into the foam to create a varied arrangement.

Harvest Festival

This magnificent autumnal arrangement is long and low in shape
and would make an excellent centrepiece for a large table.

You will need:

5 bunches artificial grapes
1 bunch *Ambrosinia*
36 assorted roses
35-40 poppy seedheads
11 stems artificial berries
5 stems white paper flowers

Instructions

Pack a low dish or tray with a shallow, but full-width, piece of foam. If you have trouble finding a piece of foam of the right dimensions then cut a large piece in half. Cover lightly with moss, then secure both the foam and the moss to the container with florist's tape. Wire the flowers with 22 gauge stem wires. To wire the artificial grapes use 18 gauge wire, first dipping the end into a latex-based adhesive and then pressing it firmly into the fruit. Cover all the wires with stem binding tape. Leave the artificial berries and white paper flowers on their original stems. Use the flowers to create the basic outline of the arrangement, inserting them into the sides of the foam at either end of the base. Add the berries, placing two – one shorter than the other – at each end, two along each side and three on top of the foam. Fill in with remaining material, creating a luxuriant display.

Topiary

*This unusual foliage topiary is made using attractive
silver blue-green Eucalyptus leaves.*

Eucalyptus Tree in Terracotta Pot

You will need:

3 branches 2.5 cm (1 in) in diameter and
25 cm (10 in) in length
1 foam ball
8 bunches glycerined *Eucalyptus*
A little bung or lychin moss

Instructions

Begin by placing some stones in the bottom of a medium-sized terracotta pot, and then fill it three-quarters full with quick drying plaster. Set the three branches in the centre of the pot and wire them together at the top and bottom. Quick drying plaster does harden in a very short space of time, so it is important to work quickly. Take a dry foam ball and cut a hole in it the same size as the circumference of the trunk and about 5 cm (2 in) in depth. Cover the foam ball with a piece of wire netting, making sure that the hole is kept clear. Squeeze some glue into the hole and push the foam ball onto the trunk. Leave it to dry. Thread a 22 gauge wire through part of the netting at the base of the ball and wind it around the trunk. Twist the ends tightly to secure. Do this at equal intervals around the trunk, making sure that the ball is firmly attached. Cut the stems of *Eucalyptus* into short lengths. Make sure that you cut as close as possible to the next set of leaves, as this enables the whole stem to be used. Wire the *Eucalyptus* pieces together in bunches of three (page 11), using 22 gauge wire, and trim any excess leaving a clear 5 cm (2 in) of stem. Cover the foam ball with the *Eucalyptus* bunches. Start working from the top, keeping the bunches as close together as possible. Turn the pot frequently, making sure that the effect is even. Finally, lightly cover the plaster with the moss.

Large Arrangements

*D*ried flowers can be used to create magnificent formal displays. Though these more complex arrangements will take time to make, they will be well worth the effort.

Lavender Vase

Dried lavender makes a simple arrangement with a light, fresh fragrance. Here, it is arranged to maximum effect in a classical urn.

You will need:
> 6 bunches lavender

Instructions

Cut a piece of dry foam, making sure that it is a fraction bigger than the neck of the container. Push it into place, leaving at least half of the block above the rim. Use a craft knife to shape the block, rounding off the corners. Divide each lavender bunch into 4 and trim stems to 10-12.5 cm (4-5 in) in length. Wire with 22 gauge wires and bind with stem binding tape (page 11). Beginning at the top, push the lavender securely into place. Work downwards, keeping the bunches tightly packed.

Spring Arrangement

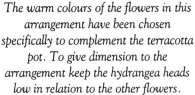

The warm colours of the flowers in this arrangement have been chosen specifically to complement the terracotta pot. To give dimension to the arrangement keep the hydrangea heads low in relation to the other flowers.

You will need:

2 bunches *Ambrosinia*
2 bunches scabious
20 stems large roses
8 stems yellow kangaroo paws
4 heads hydrangea

Instructions

Wire the flowers into small bunches using 22 gauge stem wires and cover with stem binding tape. Cut a piece of dry foam to fit snugly into the container, making sure that it sits slightly above the rim. Cover this with moss and secure with florist's tape. Create the basic shape of the arrangement, positioning bunches in the centre and around the edges of the foam. Intersperse hydrangea heads, making sure that their stems are slightly shorter than the other flowers. Make sure that they are positioned quite low in the arrangement, as this will maintain the overall balance of the display.

Fan-Shaped Display

Using a wide range of colours and textures, this sumptuous arrangement looks
magnificent in an empty fireplace or against a wall and is ideal for
a special occasion. It is a facing, rather than an all-round, arrangement and is designed to
be viewed from the front or the sides.

You will need:
5 bunches cones
4 bunches peach roses
3-5 bunches marjoram
3 bunches assorted roses
2 bunches mixed species roses
2 bunches green golden rod
15 cinnamon sticks
7 heads hydrangea
5 stems artificial fruits
1 metre (1⅛ yd) silk

Instructions

Pack the container with dry foam, making sure that it fits securely. Cover it lightly with moss and use florist's tape to secure. Cut the silk into nine squares. Make soft fabric 'balloons' from these pieces by bringing the corners together, pinching them tightly with your fingers, and binding with silver wire. Wire each fabric piece to green cane using 22 gauge wire, tucking in any rough edges as you go. Bind with stem binding tape.

Wire the cinnamon sticks. To do this put two or three in your hand and roll them so that they fit together quite closely. Then wind a wire around the centre, so that it is tight enough to cut into the bark very slightly, and twist the ends together to secure. Wire the cones, circling a wire around the base of each, making sure that it is caught between the scales, and twisting the ends to secure. Small and medium sized cones can be wired on 22 gauge wires, though for larger cones it is advisable to use 18 gauge wires. Wire the flowers into small bunches and the artificial fruits singly. Secure bunches of flowers, fruits, cones and cinnamon sticks onto canes with wire.

This arrangement is worked from the back of the container to the front. Begin by placing the first bunch of flowers three-quarters of the way back from front edge. Place bunches around outer edge and middle of the foam, using them to build up the basic framework of the arrangement. Fill in with other canes pushing some deeper into the foam to give dimension.

Silk Flowers

*T*he wide range of realistic-looking silk flowers now available on the market can be used to create lasting displays.

Peach Silk Flowers

Peach roses have been combined with white daisies and small sprays of peach and white flowers to make a compact, elegant arrangement, that looks good on a windowsill.

You will need:
3-4 large silk roses
4-5 silk roses in bud
7 large silk daisies
3 sprays small silk flowers
Grasses

Instructions

Choose a small container with a wide rim, pack it with dry foam and use florist's tape to secure. Use the roses to create the basic structure of the arrangement. Place two tall stems at the centre of the foam, and then work evenly on both sides to create a fan shape, ensuring that the flower heads of the final stems fall below the rim of the container. This is important as it will ensure that the display looks balanced. Add the daisies, using them to flesh out the basic shape. Push their stems deeper into the foam as this will give the arrangement more depth. Use the small sprays of peach and white flowers to fill any gaps. Finally add the blades of grass, using them to break the outline slightly.

Silk Aquilegia

Often the smallest silk flowers are the most realistic. Here, silk aquilegia and soft, drooping blossom have been combined in a subtle, delicate arrangement, reminiscent of spring.

You will need:
Silk Aquilegia
Silk apple or cherry blossom

Instructions
Cut a small piece of dry foam and push it into the neck of the vase, leaving about 2.5 cm (1 in) above the rim. Begin by pushing the stems of blossom firmly into the foam, bending the wires to create the required shape. Then add the silk aquilegia, cutting the stems shorter and placing them closer to the heart of the arrangement, giving it its depth.

Cerise Chrysanthemums

Silk chrysanthemums in a deep cerise pink have been used to maximum effect in this charming triangular-shaped arrangement.

You will need:
15 silk chrysanthemums

Instructions

Take a small, shallow bowl and pack it with dry foam. Use florist's tape to secure. Begin by setting the outline of the arrangement, placing a tall stem at the centre back and then a stem at each side of the base. Build up the triangular shape of the arrangement, making sure that both sides are even. Cut the stems of some of the blooms quite short and use these to fill the arrangement out, giving it body.

Yellow & Gold Display

In this gold and yellow arrangement an informal, natural feeling has been achieved by letting stems droop loosely over the edge of the container. Touches of white add freshness and definition.

You will need:
8 gold silk chrysanthemums
8 pale yellow silk chrysanthemums
15-20 gold silk carnations
15-20 pale yellow silk carnations
3 sprays small white silk flowers

Instructions
Position a piece of dry foam in the neck of the vase, making sure that it sits above the rim. Using a selection of silk blooms in complementary yellows and golds, begin to construct the outline of the arrangement. Use a few blooms to set the height and width of the display. Gradually fill out this outline, making sure that the display is well balanced. Ensure that a few blooms are positioned below the rim of the container to soften the effect.

Yellow Chrysanthemums

Yellow silk chrysanthemums have been arranged in a deep wicker basket, making a colourful, realistic display, that fills an empty summer fireplace perfectly.

You will need:
30-40 yellow silk chrysanthemums

Instructions
Begin by covering the top of the basket with crumpled wire mesh, securing it firmly to the sides of the basket with wire. With a few stems set the basic outline of the arrangement, defining the height and the width that you require. Once this fan-shape has been created, then add the remaining blooms, pushing them further through the wire to give the display depth. Cut the wires of some of the blooms shorter than others, and use these to soften the arrangement at the front, bending the stems over the rim of the basket and ensuring that the flower heads are facing forward.

Poppies and Cornflowers

Brilliant red poppies and very realistic cornflowers have been combined with pretty white and silver foliage to make a vibrant and unstructured display.

You will need:
10 silk poppies
15-20 cornflowers
Assorted foliage

Instructions

Choose a narrow necked container, such as this shiny brass jug. Begin by placing the poppies in the container, using the larger blooms to create a focal point for the arrangement. Then add the cornflowers, placing them close quite close to the poppies – this will make a good contrast, emphasising the colours of both types of flower. Finally, add the foliage, using it to soften the effect of the display.

Silk Anemones

Red, white and pink silk anemones and white gypsophila are used to great effect in this simple windowsill arrangement.

You will need:
14 silk anemones
3 sprays silk gypsophila

Instructions
Cut a piece of dry foam a little larger than the neck of the vase, and push it into place. The foam should sit a little higher than the rim of the container. Cover the foam with a thin covering of moss and secure it with wire pins. To make these pins cut 18 or 22 gauge wire into short pieces and bend them in half. Pins are almost invisible and they should be used in any arrangement where florist's tape would show. Then push the silk anemones firmly into the foam, making a low, domed arrangement. Try to ensure a good mix of colours. Finally add the sprays of gypsophila, using them to soften the overall effect.

Drying Guide

The following plants are suitable for air drying:

Acanthus
Achillea
Acroclinium
Anaphalis
Astilbe
Bamboo
Barley
Bells of Ireland
Bottlebrush
Borage
Buddleia
Burdock
Chamomile
Chinese lantern
Chive
Clary
Cornflower
Cow parsley seedheads
Delphinium
Dill
Dock
Eucalyptus leaves
Feverfew

Fox glove seedheads
French marigold
Gladioli seedheads
Globe thistle seedheads
Golden rod
Grasses
Gypsophila
Heather
Helichrysum
Helipterum
Hogweed seedheads
Hollyhock seedheads
Honesty seedheads
Hydrangea
Iris seedheads
Lady's mantle
Larkspur
Lavender
Lotus seedheads
Love-in-a-mist
Lupin seedheads
Mimosa
Monkshood

Oats
Onion seedheads
Poppy seedheads
Protea
Rhodanthe
Rose
Rose-bay willowherb
Sage
Scabious
Sea holly
Sedum
Sea lavender
Shepherd's purse
Statice
Sunray
Sweetcorn
Sweet William
Tansy
Teasel seedheads
Thistle seedheads
Veronica
Wheat
Xeranthemum